Groups 4 Health

TREATMENTS THAT WORK

TREATMENTS THAT WORK

G4H
Groups for Health

Groups 4 Health

Managing Loneliness and Social Disconnection

PARTICIPANT WORKBOOK

CATHERINE HASLAM
TEGAN CRUWYS
SARAH V. BENTLEY
JOLANDA JETTEN
S. ALEXANDER HASLAM

OXFORD
UNIVERSITY PRESS

OXFORD
UNIVERSITY PRESS

Oxford University Press is a department of the University of Oxford. It furthers the University's objective of excellence in research, scholarship, and education by publishing worldwide. Oxford is a registered trade mark of Oxford University Press in the UK and certain other countries.

Published in the United States of America by Oxford University Press
198 Madison Avenue, New York, NY 10016, United States of America.

CIP data is on file at the Library of Congress

ISBN 978–0–19–777677–3

DOI: 10.1093/med-psych/9780197776773.001.0001

The manufacturer's authorised representative in the EU for product safety is Oxford University Press España S.A. of el Parque Empresarial San Fernando de Henares, Avenida de Castilla, 2 – 28830 Madrid (www.oup.es/en).

About ✓TREATMENTS THAT WORK™

One of the most difficult problems confronting patients with various disorders and diseases is finding the best help available. Everyone is aware of friends or family who have sought treatment from a seemingly reputable practitioner, only to find out later from another doctor that the original diagnosis was wrong or the treatments recommended were inappropriate or perhaps even harmful. Most patients, or family members, address this problem by reading everything they can about their symptoms, seeking out information on the internet or aggressively "asking around" to tap knowledge from friends and acquaintances. Governments and health care policymakers are also aware that people in need do not always get the best treatments—something they refer to as *variability in health care practices.*

Now health care systems around the world are attempting to correct this variability by introducing *evidence-based practice*. This simply means that it is in everyone's interest that people get the most up-to-date and effective care for a particular problem. Health care policymakers have also recognized that it is very useful to give consumers of health care as much information as possible, so that they can make intelligent decisions in a collaborative effort to improve health and well-being. This series, Treatments *That Work*, is designed to accomplish just that. Only the latest and most effective interventions for particular problems are described, in user-friendly language. To be included in this series, each treatment program must pass the highest standards of evidence available, as determined by a scientific advisory board. Thus, when individuals suffering from these problems or their family members seek out an expert clinician who is familiar with these interventions and decides that they are appropriate, people will have confidence they are receiving the best care available. Of course, only your health care professional can decide on the right mix of treatments for you.

Loneliness and social disconnection is something that many people experience. However, it is something that people are particularly likely to experience when they are going through a life transition of some form—going to college, leaving home, becoming a parent, having a serious illness, getting divorced, or retiring from work. These are points at which our social relationships can undergo significant change, and this has consequences for our sense of place in the world. In such contexts, loneliness is a signal that something is missing in our social relationships and connections and that these are in need of attention. Where this feeling persists, our mental and physical health can really suffer.

Groups 4 Health directly addresses this need. Through the range of activities in this five-session program, participants are supported to develop the knowledge and skills they need to build, sustain, and independently manage these relationships in positive ways both in the present and into the future. This Participant Workbook functions as a resource for participants—providing a record of activities and a summary of what they will have learned as they work through the program. Groups 4 Health challenges and empowers people to harness and optimize positive social connections, which has a hugely important role to play in the prevention and management of the burden of loneliness. In the face of the current global loneliness pandemic, it is a program for our times.

David H. Barlow, Editor-in-Chief,
Treatments *ThatWork*™
Boston, MA

Contents

Introduction to Groups 4 Health

The Groups 4 Health Program . . . How Does It All Fit Together?

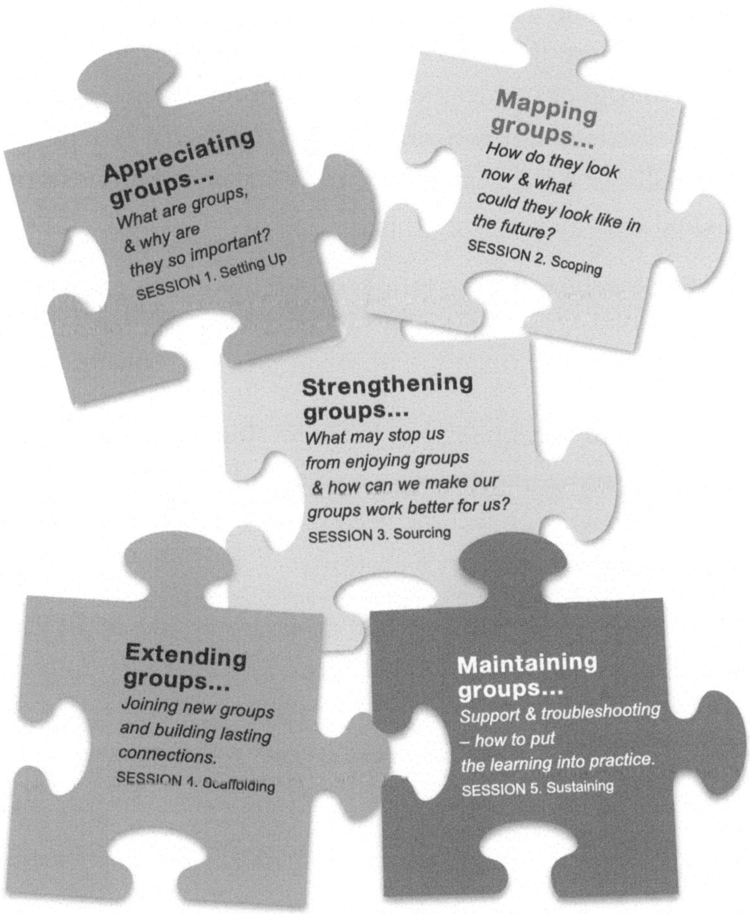

Figure I.1:
Groups 4 Health program elements

What Is Groups 4 Health and Why Do We Need It?

Social interaction is what makes us human. Along these lines, many of us see and interact with other people most days. We do this at home, in the workplace, and in a range of settings within our various neighborhoods and communities. We also interact with others in a range of roles—for example, as friends, as parents, as colleagues, as neighbors, as members of a religious organization, and so on.

Feeling positively connected to other people helps us to feel part of something, as well as providing us with support, meaning, and purpose. Evidence also suggests that it is these positive group memberships that keep us happy and healthy.

But it is easy to take our membership in groups for granted and to overlook the importance of group life. There are also times in our lives when it is hard to do what we need to do to stay connected. This is where Groups 4 Health comes in. Through this program you will learn:

- what makes up a social group,
- how social groups make a difference to our lives and to our health in general,
- ways to help us stay connected to the groups that are important to us,
- ways to extend our network and join new social groups, and
- the skills we need to manage these social connections to make sure they work for us and last.

This will be achieved over four sessions, with one additional follow-up session to check how things are going and to ensure that your social relationships are meeting your needs.

This Participant Workbook has been developed to support you in working through the program, providing you with a record of your thoughts and experiences. You can revisit it whenever you feel the need to think again about some of the things we have learned and talked about as a group.

[Activity sheets from the Workbook can also be accessed by searching for this book's title on the Oxford Academic platform, at academic.oup.com.]

CHAPTER 1

Session 1
Setting Up: Appreciating Groups

SESSION AIMS

1. To get to know one another.
2. To raise awareness of the role that social groups play in our lives.
3. To learn about the health benefits of social group membership.
4. To discover how social groups can be a psychological resource.

Connections Between You and the People in Your Life

Groups 4 Health is all about making connections. So let's start by connecting with this group first, to say hello and introduce ourselves.

Activity 1.1: What Is Important to You?

In an ideal world, we want a good fit between our sense of who we are and the people who are in our lives. That is, you want the people in your life—the groups in your life—to be a reflection of you and how you want to be.

A good way to check in on this is to think about what the important parts of yourself are. Activity 1.1 will help you do that.

First, let's think about what's important to you. This could include your . . .

Interests (reading, listening to music, keeping up with current affairs)

Values (honesty, fairness, caring)

Personality (you like to meet people, you're quiet, you like to laugh)

Activities (going to the movies, cooking)

Beliefs (religious, spiritual, diversity)

Aspirations (to learn, to try something new)

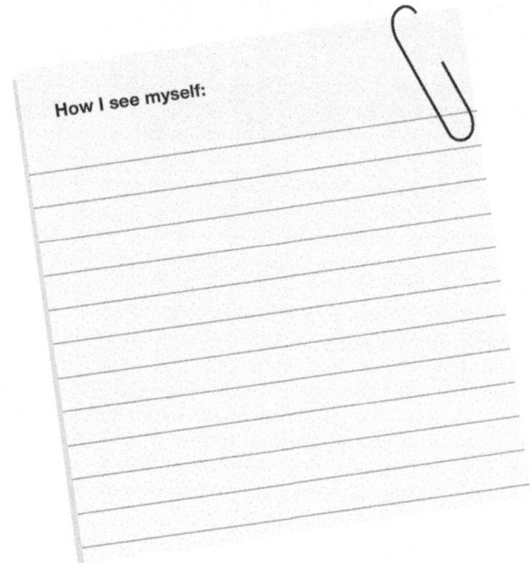

Now, write down what's important to you in the space provided on the notepad above.

Creating a Self-Aspect Pie

Now we're going to get you to create a "self-aspect pie." For each aspect of yourself that you have written down, think about how important this is to how you see yourself. In the pie, very important parts of you should be bigger slices and less important parts should be smaller. Take a look at the examples in Figures 1.1 and 1.2, and then make your own self-aspect pie in Activity 1.2: Your Self-Aspect Pie.

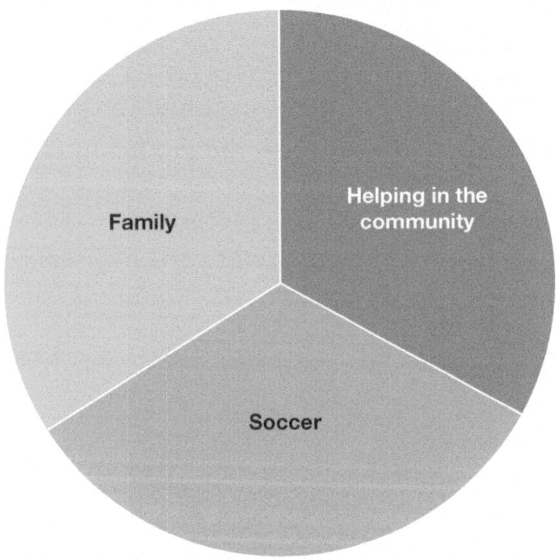

Figure 1.1:

Kim's self-aspect pie

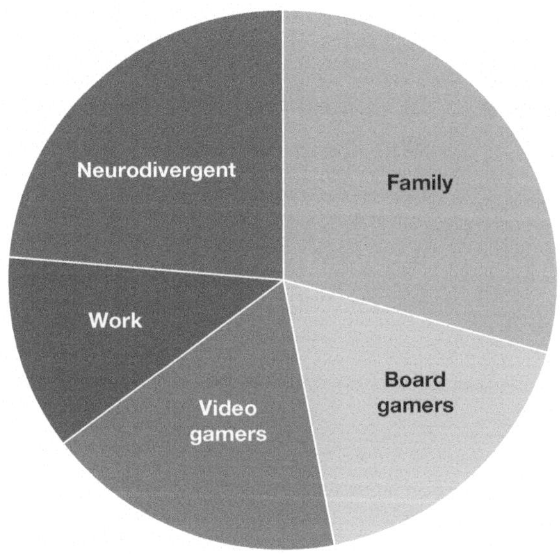

Figure 1.2:

Rowan's self-aspect pie

Activity 1.2: Your Self-Aspect Pie

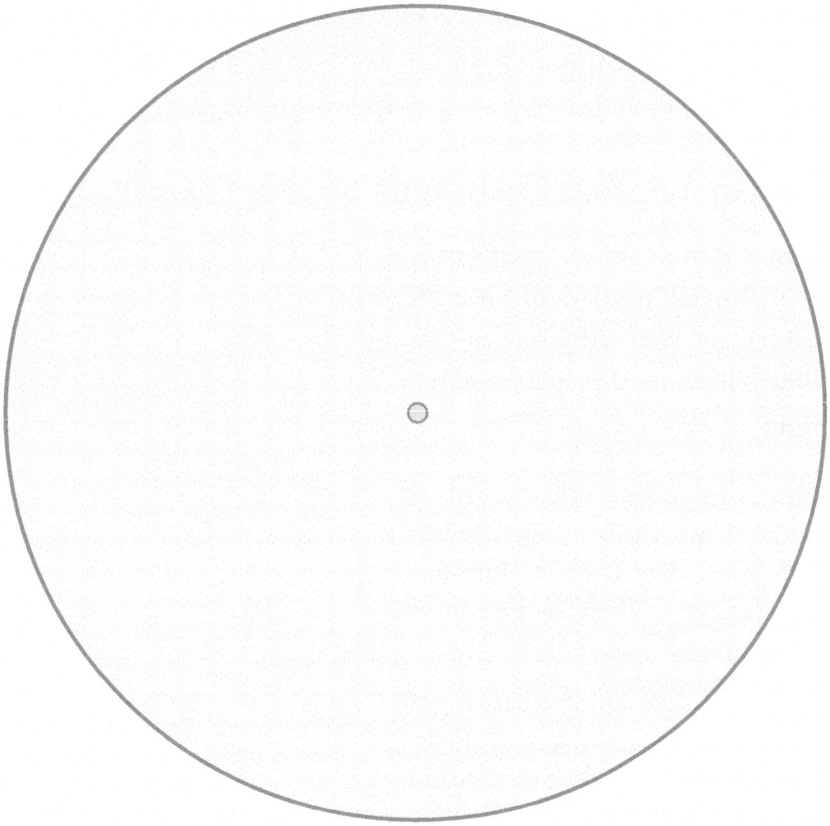

Reflecting and Connecting

Self-aspect pies help to illustrate the different aspects of ourselves and how important they are in our lives. By thinking about these self-aspects, we can also find common ground with other people who might share our interests, goals, or beliefs.

Turn to your neighbor now and talk with them about one or two of the self-aspects they listed in their self-aspect pie, and one or two that you listed.

When you have exchanged thoughts, we will ask you to re-introduce your neighbor to the others in the group, and they can re-introduce you.

Working Together

The aim of these sessions is to talk, share, and learn. This is much easier to do when we share some common ground. So, let's think about some of the interests, goals, aspirations, or activities that we share within the group.

Activity 1.3: Your Goals, Your Neighbor's Goals, Your Group's Goals

First, think about your own goals for taking part in Groups 4 Health, and write one or two down here in the space on the right.

Next, turn to your other neighbor, and talk with them about one or two goals they have for Groups 4 Health. Then write these down too.

Now let's talk about what might be some of the shared goals, interests, or activities within this group.

Make sure you have taken notes in the space to the right.

My goals:

My neighbor's goals:

My group's goals:

What Do We Believe Is Good for Our Health?

It's fair to say that we are bombarded with information about all the things we should do to keep ourselves healthy. So, what are the things that are important for good health?

Activity 1.4: Ranking Health Factors

As a group, let's take a moment to rank a set of factors for their importance to our health. The health factors are listed in the left-hand column of Table 1.1 in no particular order. So let's rank them based on what we think are most important for staying healthy.

Table 1.1 Health ranking task

Health factors	Rank the importance of each factor from 1 through 11
Taking appropriate medication	
Being socially integrated	
Not drinking excessive alcohol	
Receiving social support	
Not being exposed to air pollution	
Having flu vaccination	
Not smoking	
Quitting smoking	
Not higher weight	
Exercising	
Being physically active	

A ranking of 1 indicates the most important factor for health, and a ranking of 11 indicates the least important.

Now that we have ranked these different health factors, let's look at Figure 1.3, which shows what other people in the general public thought when asked to do the same thing.

As you can see from Figure 1.3, people ranked things like not smoking, exercise, physical activity, and weight as the most important factors. Does this match your group's ratings?

Now let's look at the white circles on Figure 1.4, to see what the real rankings are based on the latest research. Contrary to what a lot of people think, you can see that social support and social integration are actually at the top of the list (not at the bottom where the general public placed them) and that they are more important for health than all of the other factors here.

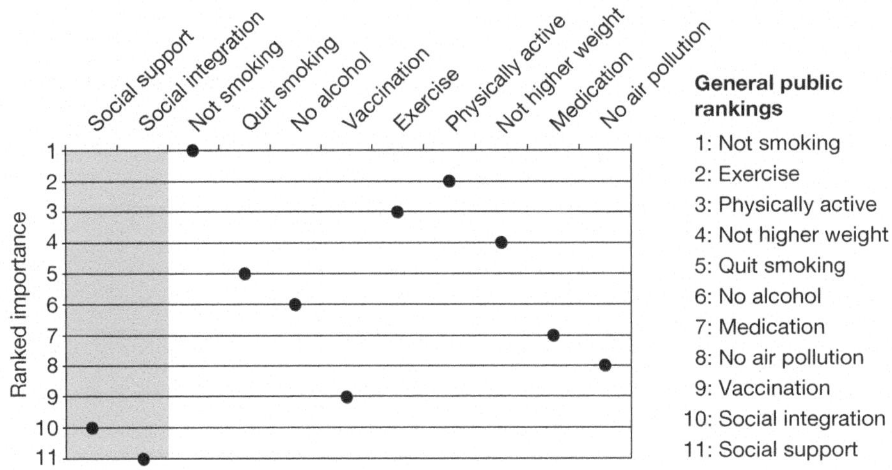

Figure 1.3:
General public health rankings

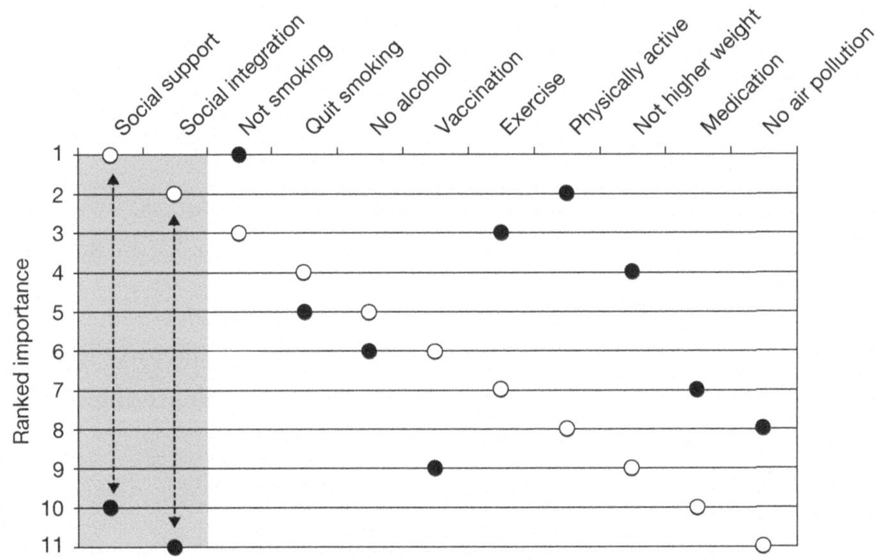

Figure 1.4:
Health rankings from the general public and research studies

Social Relationships Protect Health

Our social relationships keep us healthy. We know that people who are more socially connected are healthier and happier, and they also live longer. In contrast, people who are socially disconnected generally have poorer mental health and take longer to recover from illness. You can see some of the benefits of high social connection and the dangers of low social connection in Figure 1.5.

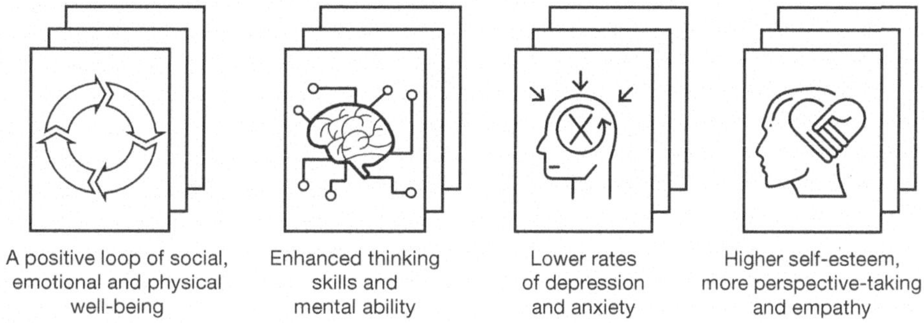

Figure 1.5:

The benefits of social connectedness

What Makes a Group?

Now we know that social relationships and groups are good for our health. But what counts as a group? When you think of social groups, who and what do you think of?

Activity 1.5: What Kinds of Social Groups Are Out There?

When we talk about social groups, what do we mean? A social group is made up of people who matter to us and with whom we bond. A social group could be with one other person or with hundreds of other people. It could take the form of a family group, a sports group, an informal coffee group, or formal membership of a club or association. A group can also be based on shared beliefs, common roles, or similar perspectives—as a vegetarian, a Christian, a parent, or a basketball team fan. All these different social connections form our social worlds and in turn, they all shape who we are as individuals.

Use the space below to write some examples of groups that we come up with.

What kinds of social groups are out there?

Now that we've thought about the different social groups that exist, let's take this a step further to think about the groups that are part of *your* life.

Activity 1.6: Groups in Your Life

In the box below, list all the groups that *you* belong to.

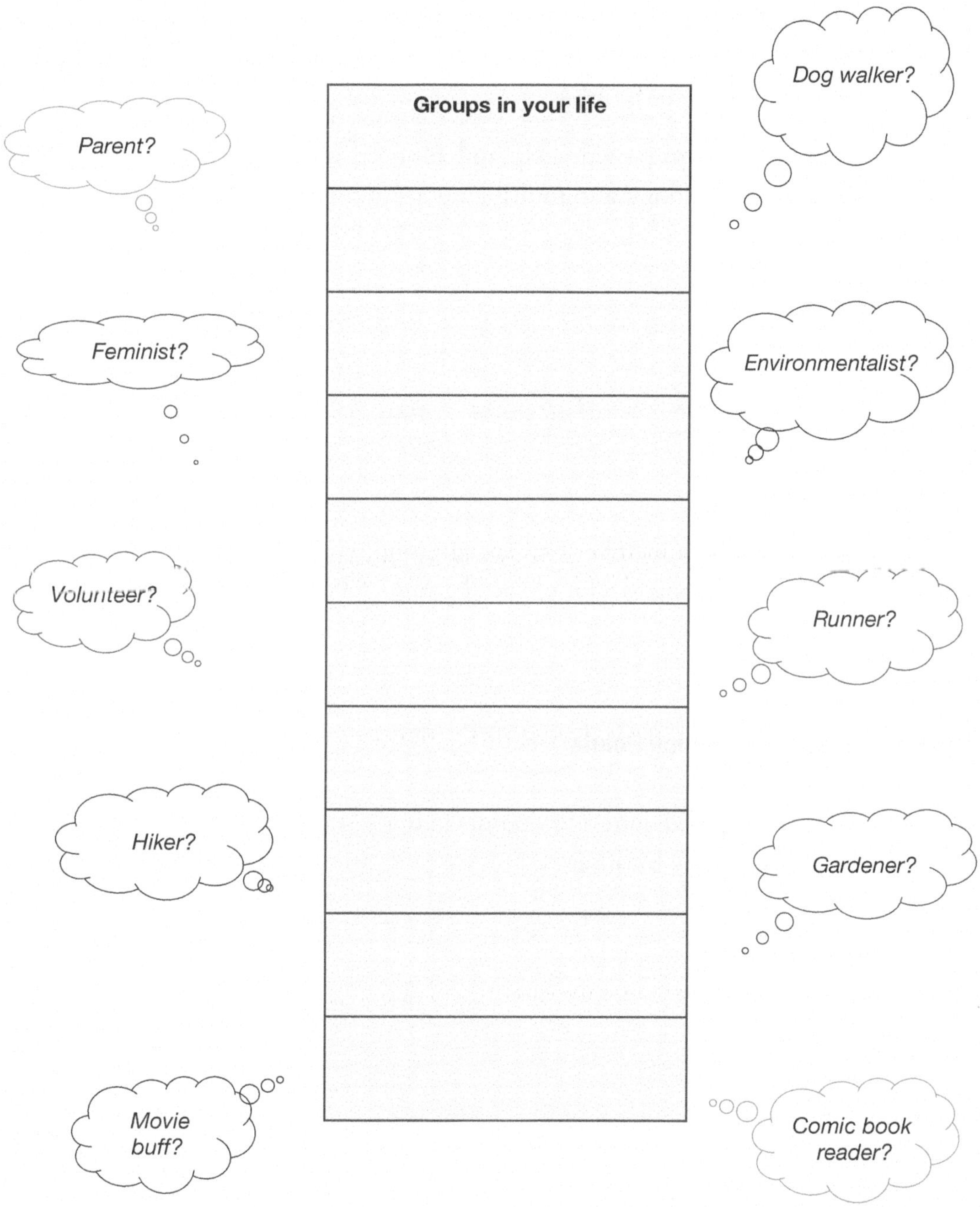

Social Groups Are a Psychological Resource

We can think of the health benefits of social groups as working like a multivitamin. Vitamin A (which we get from green vegetables and various fruits) helps strengthen bones and teeth, Vitamin B (from meat, fish, and mushrooms) helps brain function, and Vitamin C (from citrus fruit) helps the body heal. We know that without a good range of vitamins, we would get very sick.

Social groups are also essential to our health, keeping our minds and bodies working normally, and buffering us from the effects of various forms of stress. In this way, social groups are as much of a resource as vitamins or medicine—and they have a big role to play in keeping us healthy.

Different groups provide help and support in different ways and at different times. This is why belonging to multiple social groups is so important.

One social group = one psychological resource

Multiple social groups = multiple psychological resources

So, if you are a member of a social group, you have access to some social resources, and if you belong to a lot of social groups then you have access to a lot more psychological resources.

Session Summary: Learning Points

We have covered quite a few points in our session today, and it is useful to keep a summary of our key learnings.

Activity 1.7: Learning Points from Today's Session

Use the space below to write down some learning points from today's session.

Learning points from today's session:

Reflection Task

This reflection task is for you to complete before the next session.

In this activity you will be asked to think about any challenges you have experienced either in the past, or between now and the next session. Then think about the different ways that the people around you either helped you, or could have helped you, to reduce or overcome these challenges.

Activity 1.8: Challenging Moments

The space below is for you to write down some of your thoughts about these challenges and ways to overcome them. Bring this along next time, and we'll use this to start discussions in the next session.

Challenging moments	*How my social groups helped or could have helped, to reduce the impact of the challenge*

CHAPTER 2 Session 2 Scoping: Mapping Groups

SESSION AIMS

1. To raise awareness of our social groups.
2. To raise awareness of the different relationships between us and the groups in our social world.
3. To achieve awareness through creating a social identity map.

Review and Check-In

How did the reflection task go? What were some of the key points that came up in discussion? There is space below to write some of these down.

....

....

....

....

Mapping Your Social World

As we talked about last time, our social groups are an important psychological resource—like vitamins or medicine, or even like a pacemaker that keeps our heart beating regularly. In the same way, our social groups act like a medicine, and this helps us to stay healthy.

To make best use of this resource we need to know who is part of our social world and to understand the role they play in it. Social identity mapping helps us to do this.

Social Identity Mapping

Before we get started making our own social identity maps, it can be helpful to take a look at some examples. The maps in Figures 2.1 and 2.2 show Kim and Rowan's connections with their social groups, how important each group is, and how compatible the groups are with each other.

Everyone's map is unique because our social worlds are diverse.

There is no "right map." The important thing is to find what is right for *you*.

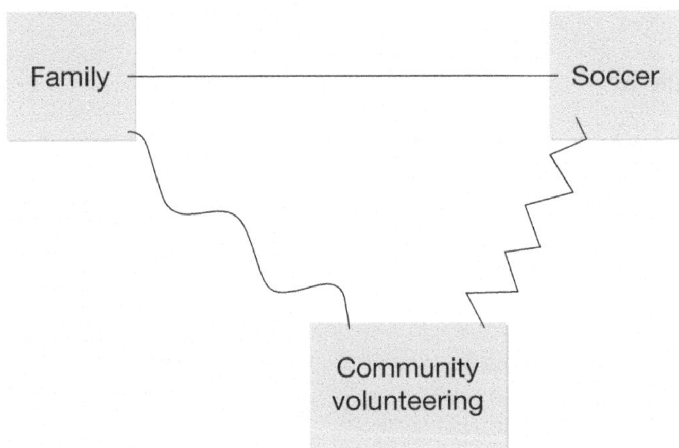

Figure 2.1:
Kim's social identity map

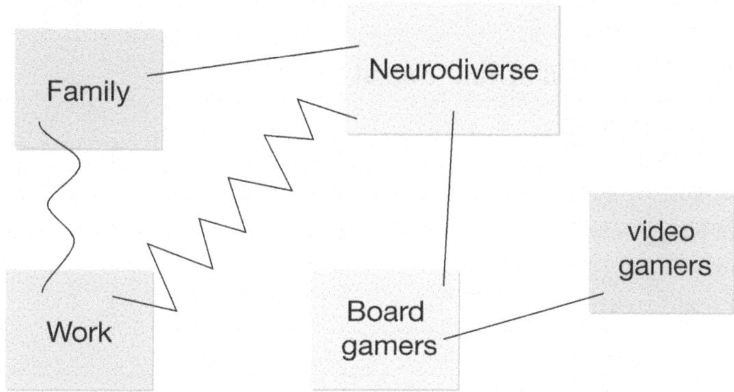

Figure 2.2:
Rowan's social identity map

Now that you have seen some examples, try making your own social identity map. In this exercise, the focus is on *your* social world and understanding what it looks like right now.

Activity 2.1: Create Your Own Social Identity Map

Use the following step-by-step guide to **create your own social identity map**. You should do this on the large sheet of paper and Post-it Notes that your facilitator provided. After you have created your map, there is a page in this Workbook, after the mapping instructions, where you can tape or paste your completed map so it is easy to find.

Stage 1

Naming Your Groups and Rating Their Importance

In the last session, you identified the various social groups that you belong to (in Activity 1.6 on page 12 of the Workbook). To start the process of social identity mapping, write down each of these groups on a separate Post-it Note, based on how important they are to you. Add in any other groups that you have thought of since then.

Remember, the size of the Post-it Note matters!

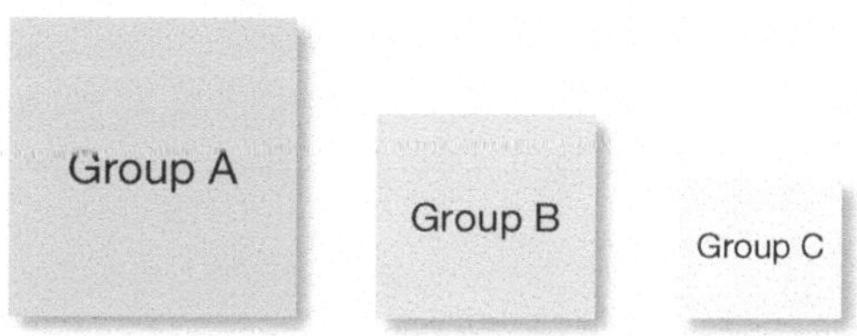

Put the name of each very important group on a large Post-it Note, the name of each moderately important group on a medium-sized Post-it Note, and the name of each less important group on a small Post-it Note.

Stage 2

How Typical Are You of Your Social Groups?

For each group, indicate how typical you are of the group and the people in it. Put this rating in the top left corner of each Post-it Note.

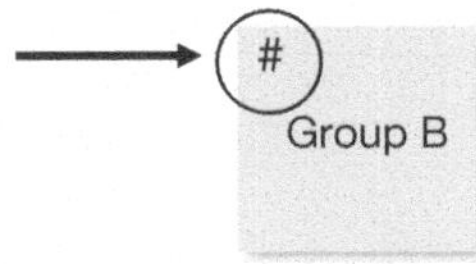

Use a scale from 1 to 10:

1 .... 2 .... 3 .... 4 .... 5 .... 6 .... 7 .... 8 .... 9 10	
Not typical	Very typical

Stage 3

Your Group Participation

How many days in an average month do you see or do things with each group? If it's every day, the number would be 30. If it's every week, then the number would be 4. So, the range is 0 to 30.

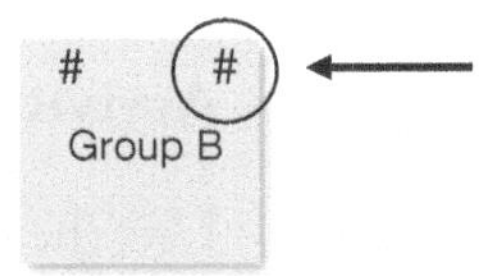

Write this number for each group in the top right corner of each Post-it Note.

Stage 4

Support from Your Groups

Now, rate how much support you get from each group. Rate this on a scale from 1 (*no support at all*) to 10 (*a very high level of support*). For example, you could belong to a work-related group or a family-related group that provides you with a lot of practical support or emotional support, so the rating you might give that group would be high, for instance an 8 or a 9. For every group, write your rating in the bottom right corner of each Post-it Note.

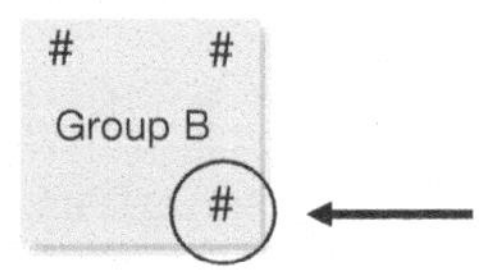

Use a scale from 1 to 10:

1 .... 2 .... 3 .... 4 .... 5 .... 6 .... 7 .... 8 .... 9 10	
No support at all	A very high level of support

Stage 5

Positivity of Your Group Memberships

Rate how positive you feel about being part of each group. Write your rating in the bottom left corner of each Post-it Note.

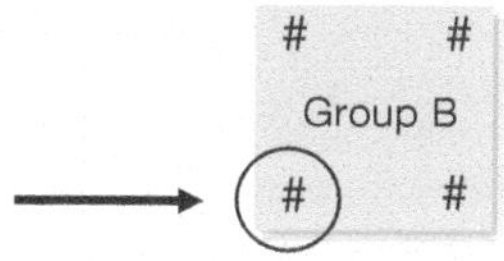

Use a scale from 1 to 10:

1 .... 2 .... 3 .... 4 .... 5 .... 6 .... 7 .... 8 .... 9 10	
Not at all positive	Very positive

Stage 6

Group Similarity

We know that some groups are very similar to each other because, for example, they like or do similar things. But others are very different from each other. On the large sheet of paper given to you by the group facilitators, we would like you to show how similar and different your groups are to each other. Do this by placing your Post-it Notes close together if the groups on them are similar, and farther apart if they are different. So, if two groups are very similar to each other, place these close to each other, like this:

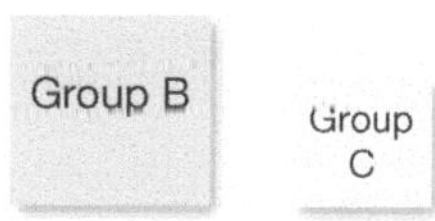

But if two groups are very different from each other (for example, they do different things, it feels different being a part of each, they have different members), place them far from each other, like this:

Stage 7

Compatibility of Your Groups

Because we typically belong to a number of groups, it can be hard at times to juggle them. In your social identity map, we would like you to use different lines to show how easy or hard it is to be part of different groups at the same time. For example, if you belong to a chess club it might be very easy to also be a member of your family, but not that easy to also be a member of your community band. Show the ease or difficulty of being part of multiple groups at the same time by using different types of lines.

If two groups are easy to belong to at the same time, join them with a straight line.

If two groups are moderately easy to belong to at the same time, join them with a wavy line.

If two groups are hard to belong to at the same time, join them with a jagged line.

For example:

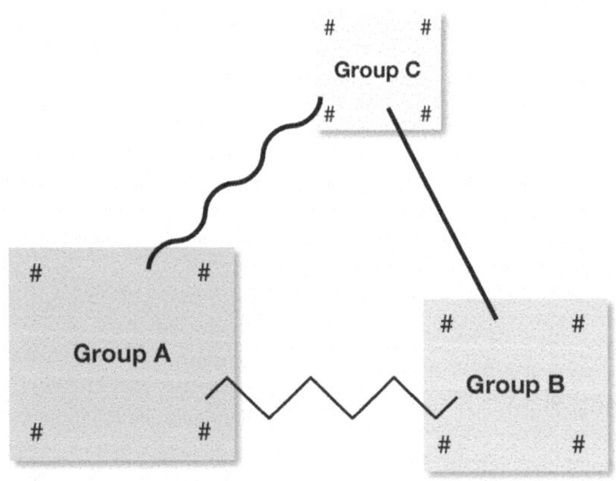

PLEASE FOLD YOUR COMPLETED MAP TO FIT THIS PAGE AND ATTACH IT HERE

Discussing Your Map

Let's talk about the maps you have created. What are some of the positive features of your maps and the relationships they highlight? Are there things in your map you are less happy about or would like to change?

"Different Groups, Different You"

One of the things that's pretty clear is that the groups that make up our identity maps can be rather diverse. This is because they might do different things, have different priorities and values, and/or get together for different reasons.

Activity 2.2: Reflecting on Your Social Identity Map

Reflecting on your social identity map, would you say that you act and behave the same with all your groups? And are there different ways in which you relate to your groups? Let's see how this plays out with our Groups 4 Health group, and with another group or two from your map. Write down these groups in the box below, and think about how you relate to each.

What are the different ways you talk, share, behave, or relate to these groups? ....

e.g., I talk about ways to connect with my Groups 4 Health group.
e.g., I talk mostly about work stuff over drinks with work friends.

With my Groups 4 Health group I...

With my .... group I...

With my .... group I...

As this shows, we don't interact (or need to interact) with all our groups in the same way. It's pretty common to engage with our groups in different ways—indeed, this it helps us to live out the different parts of ourselves with different groups.

Session Summary: Learning Points

As we did last time, let's finish by talking about some of the key learnings from today's session.

Activity 2.3: Learning Points from Today's Session

Use the space below to write down some learning points from today's session.

Learning points from today's session:

Reflection Task

This reflection task is for you to complete before the next session.

Activity 2.4: Review Your Social Identity Map

Creating a social identity map for the first time can be an interesting exercise! Before our next session, review your social identity map, and think about what's working well and less well for you.

There is space below to write down your thoughts. First, note what is working well in your map. Next, note anything you might want to adjust or change.

*What are some things that are **working well** in your map?*	
*What are some things you might like to **change** in your map?*	

CHAPTER 3 Session 3
Sourcing: Strengthening Groups

SESSION AIMS

1. To understand why we have the groups we have in our life.
2. To assess the groups we may have lost along the way.
3. To look at how we can manage challenging groups.

Review and Check-In

How did the reflection task go? What were some of the key points that came up in discussion? There is space below to write some of these down.

Understanding Our Groups

Changes in life can mean that some groups become more or less important, or we become disconnected from some groups over time. Our group connections may also change because of inevitable life events, such as moving, changing jobs, getting married, retiring, or other events and transitions. This next activity will help us think through these changes.

Activity 3.1: How Do People's Maps Come to Look the Way They Do?

Think about your own social identity map and reflect on what changes in *your* life (positive or negative) may have affected the way your map looks today.

Write down these key events of your life in the panels.

Activity 3.2: Lost and Found

When thinking about your map, did you notice that there were groups that had been important to you in the past, but that you have now lost touch with?

Of course, sometimes it makes sense to let connections go, because our lives have moved on. But there are also times when we lose contact, or see groups less often, without meaning to.

In these circumstances, it can be good to reach out and try to reconnect with these groups.

Have you had experiences of losing contact with groups, and then trying to reconnect? Write down any examples or experiences below.

Groups I have lost:

How might you reconnect with these lost groups?

Groups I have lost and re-found:

How did you reconnect with these groups?

Managing Our Groups

Sometimes managing our groups can be hard, whether dealing with group loss, group support, or group conflict. For instance, there may be times in our lives when we belong to groups that can make our lives challenging or difficult; or there may be groups that are important to us, but that are perceived by others as negative or stigmatizing; or there may be groups that we feel we give too much to.

Sometimes it's important to step back to assess the way we interact with groups.

The Importance of Giving and Receiving

There can be times when we give a lot to groups and don't seem to get much back, and there can be other times when we get so much from our group that this can make us feel too dependent. A healthy group is like a healthy plant—it needs water in the same way a group needs nurturing for it to be supportive. But nurturing is a two-way street: not only should the group nurture you, but you should also nurture the group.

Activity 3.3: Supporting Your Social Groups

The "Giving and Receiving" diagram below provides space to write down how you help one of your social groups and how members of that group help you. Identify a group from your social identity map and jot down examples of the support that you give to this group and the support that you receive from this group.

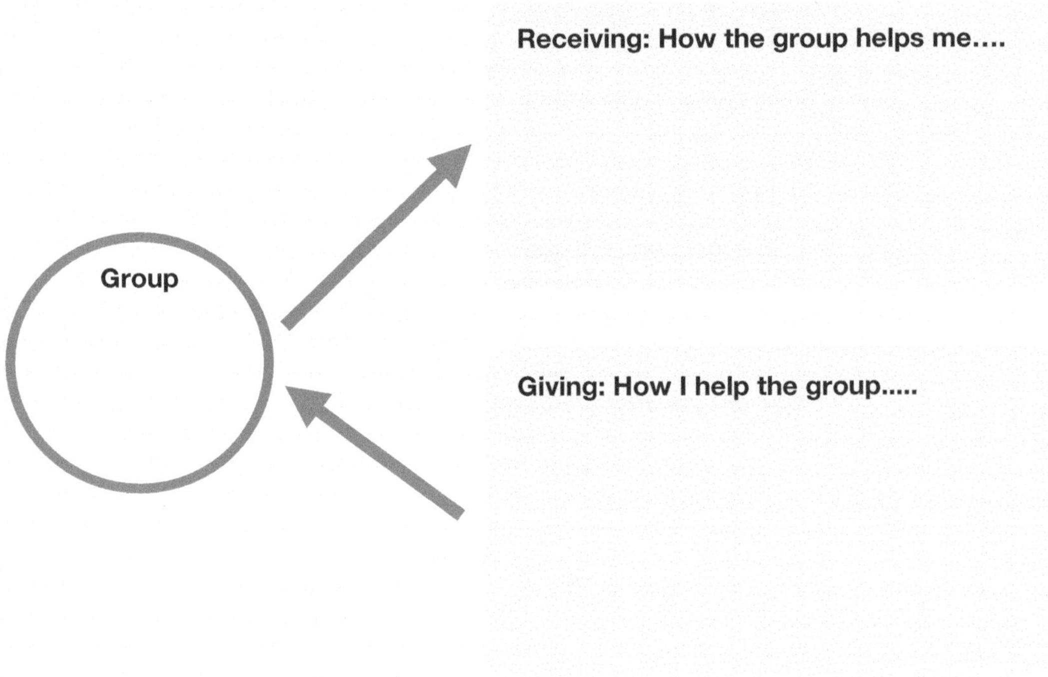

Groups That Are Challenging

Sometimes it is not easy to identify the challenging groups in your life, but there might be clues in your social identity map. In particular, the groups in your map with one or more "jagged" lines connected to them (for example, "Work" in Figure 3.1) may indicate a group that is difficult to manage.

Let's think a bit more about such challenges by looking at Figure 3.2, which is Rowan's social identity map.

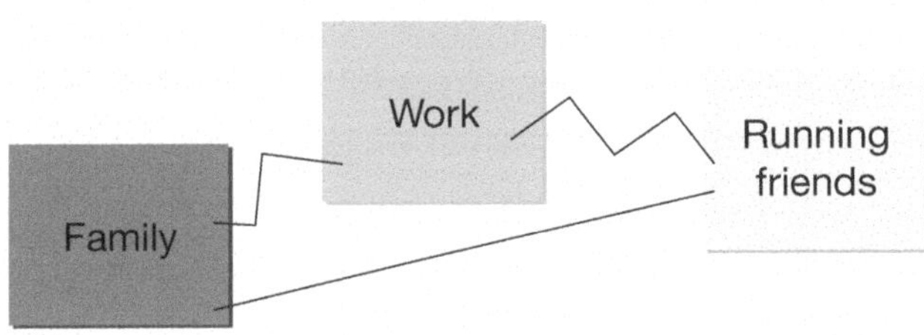

Figure 3.1:
Example social identity map

We met Rowan in earlier sessions. There are many things that Rowan's map can tell us about him, but let's think particularly about which groups might be challenging in Rowan's life.

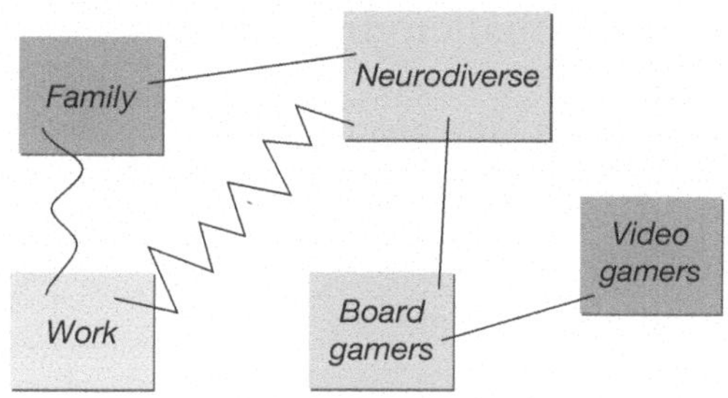

Figure 3.2:

Rowan's social identity map

Activity 3.4: Rowan's Challenging Groups

Think about the following questions, and let's discuss them together.

Rowan's challenging groups

Are there any individual groups that might be particularly challenging for Rowan? (e.g., because they might not get along with Rowan's other groups; they might be emotionally draining; they might expose Rowan to bullying; or they might be stigmatized)

Are there relationships between groups that might present challenges for Rowan?

What are some ways that Rowan might manage the group and these relationships?

Activity 3.5: Your Challenging Groups

Recognizing that challenging groups exist is an important first step. Now that we have taken a closer look at Rowan's social identity map, are there any similar challenges you see in **your** social identity map?

Use the space below to list any challenging groups in your life.

Now pair up with your neighbor and start working through these questions:

Your challenging groups

Why are these groups challenging for you?
(e.g., they don't get on with other groups in your network, they expose you to bullying, they are emotionally draining)

Do these challenging groups impact the other groups in your life?

What impact do you think these challenging groups have on your well-being?

Strategies to Help

Now, let's think about the different strategies we can use to manage groups. There are a range of different approaches we can use.

Draw on your wider network: Recognizing and drawing on a wider network of groups, particularly when they are positive, reminds us that we are not solely defined by one group. It also helps to reduce any concerns we might have about being evaluated negatively because we belong to one particular group.

Change the dynamic: Sometimes changing the group dynamic can be helpful. Changing the dynamic could involve suggesting new activities for the group, reassessing how much support you give or get from the group, bringing in new people, or reassessing how you interact with the group.

Take stock of the good and the bad: Recognizing that the groups in our lives are not perfect is important in managing expectations. Our social groups commonly have good and bad features, so accepting the group—warts and all—can be useful. Relying on, or expecting too much from, one group can also be a problem. But having access to a wider social group network helps you to spread the load.

Be socially mobile: It's important to recognize that you have some control over the groups in your life. If none of the above strategies work, you can consider spending less time with the group, perhaps temporarily or perhaps permanently. And there are times when, on balance, it's probably best to disconnect from the group entirely.

Engage in collective action: Standing together to call out experiences of poor or unfair treatment (such as exclusion or discrimination) provides a platform for mutual support and positivity. Collective action can also change how a group might be perceived by society and offer a way of giving support to others who might be facing similar challenges.

Activity 3.6: Strategies to Manage Your Challenging Groups

Take two groups from your map that can be challenging and think of what strategies might help you manage these groups.

Group:	*Strategy:*
Group:	*Strategy:*

Session Summary: Learning Points

As we did last time, let's finish by talking about some of the key learnings from today's session.

Activity 3.7: Learning Points from Today's Session

Use the space below to write down some learning points from today's session.

Learning points from today's session:

Reflection Task

This reflection task is for you to complete before the next session.

Activity 3.8: Group Conflicts and Strategies

During this session, we spent some time thinking about the different strategies to manage groups, and how you might apply these strategies to your groups.

Between now and the next session, try to act on one of the strategies you identified. This should focus on a group that can be challenging, but if there are no such groups in your life, focus on one that is important to you.

In the sections below, write down the situation and the strategy you used. How did that go?

The situation or group(s):	
What strategy did you use?	
What went well?	
Would you do anything differently next time?	

CHAPTER 4 Session 4 Scaffolding: Extending Groups

SESSION AIMS

1. To explore ideas for building shared identity.
2. To grow our confidence to join new groups.
3. To make a specific and concrete plan for social connectedness over the next month.

Review and Check-In

How did the reflection task go? What were some of the key points that came up in discussion? There is space below to write some of these down.

Building a Shared Identity

How do we strengthen our sense of connection with a group? Just like cooking from a recipe, Figure 4.1 shows four key ingredients that will help to create a strong basis for building social connections that last.

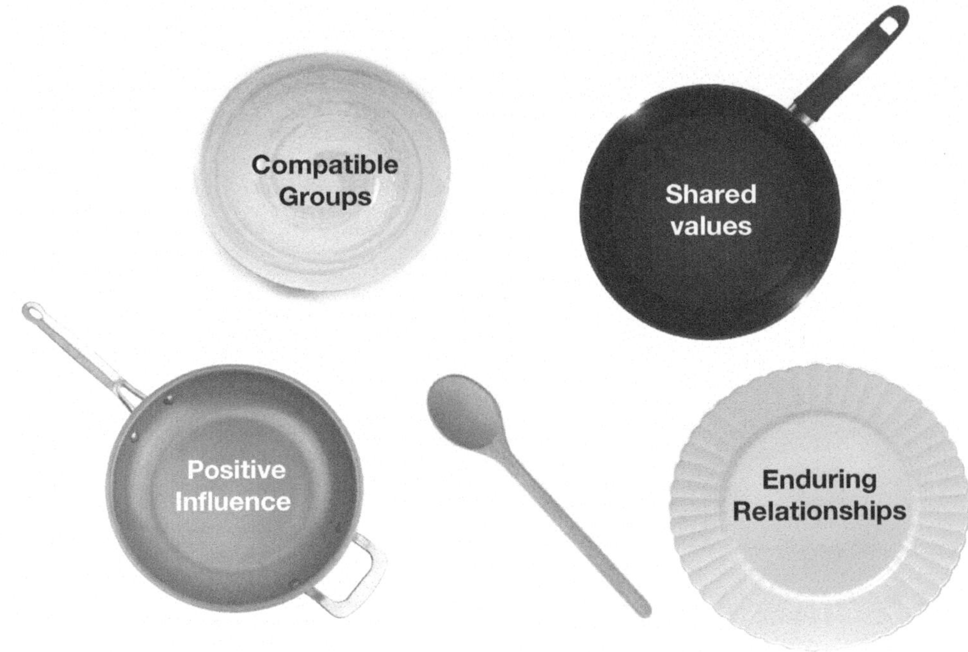

Figure 4.1:
Ingredients that help to build shared identity

1. Positive Influence

We should feel good about the group and the group should help us feel good about ourselves. Research has shown that having a positive experience with one social group—even a temporary one—makes it more likely that we will join new groups in the future and improve our health further.

A positive group experience helps us to:

1. Challenge the idea that it's hard to connect with others.
2. Learn skills that will help us to join new groups.
3. Feel more confident and comfortable in connecting with others.

What positive experiences do you have with your groups?

Turn to your neighbor and share your experiences with them.

2. Compatible Groups

We know that social groups that are compatible and a "good fit" with our other groups put less strain on us. Our groups don't have to all be the same—but it helps when we feel our groups are generally aligned. In this way, groups that fit well with each other can bring together the different aspects of who we are.

Think back to your social identity map.

Do you have any groups that are really compatible or really incompatible? Do your incompatible groups put strain on you?

Share some thoughts with your neighbor.

3. Shared Values

Values are ideas that can guide how we live our lives and help us move toward where we want to be. When those different values are shared by others around us, we feel more connected with them. Groups are also easier to maintain when they share one or more of our values (for instance, to support family, be respectful, get in shape).

Are your values shared by members of this new GROUPS 4 HEALTH group that you have joined?

Turn to your neighbor and discuss your answers together.

4. Enduring Relationships

We should feel that the group is likely to be there for us in the future. We have talked about how our social groups change over time, and this is part of the story of our lives. Research has shown that groups that stay with us through life's changes have a major impact on our health and well-being. Enduring groups are those that will be there for us now and in the future; they can help us navigate changes and challenges. Groups that we keep hold of are ones that keep on giving.

Think back to your social identity map again.

Have any of your groups been in your life for a long time? What has made these relationships endure?

Again, turn to your neighbor to discuss your answers.

Activity 4.1: What Else Might Help to Create a Good Group Connection?

Pair up with your neighbor and in the figure below, write down any other ingredients that you think might be important for creating a good group connection.

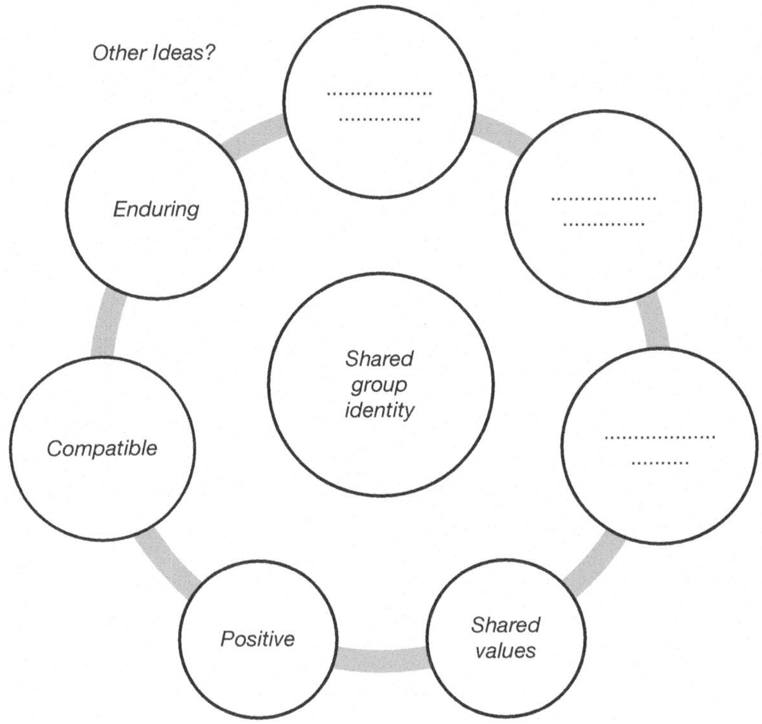

Let's discuss these ideas as a group; there is a space below where you can jot down any notes.

Learning from Our Groups 4 Health Group

You've already developed a new group in becoming part of Groups 4 Health.

Activity 4.2: Your Experiences of the Groups 4 Health Group

Let's talk about what your experience with this Groups 4 Health group has been like so far.

In the box below there is space to jot down any thoughts you have in the process of this discussion.

Your experiences of the Groups 4 Health group

How has it been so far?

Did it feel awkward or were you anxious to begin with?

What have you learned about connecting with others through this process?

The Pain Is Worth the Gain

Sometimes we might feel that reconnecting and strengthening existing connections is just too hard. We all feel this way sometimes, but if we stopped making the effort then our lives would be less rich and less healthy.

Activity 4.3: How Can Groups Help You?

Below are just some of the many things that groups can help us with. Can groups help you with any of these things right now? Put a checkmark next to the ones that apply and add any others that you think are missing from this list.

How can groups help you . . .

- ☐ Feel less stressed
- ☐ Feel less on your own
- ☐ Feel more in control of your life
- ☐ Feel more supported
- ☐ Feel more connected to other people
- ☐ To help other people more
- ☐ ______________________
- ☐ ______________________

Developing a Social Plan

Extending our social group ties can be tricky, especially knowing where to begin. To help with this, it is often useful to think about the things that are important to you as a person—as we did when you created your self-aspect pie back in Session 1. But things might have changed since then, so let's take some time to review that pie from Activity 1.2 and see if it has changed in any way.

Take a look at your pie on page 6 and consider if there are any aspects that you'd like to add or change—aspects related to interests, values, personality, activities, beliefs, and aspirations that are important to you now. You can keep these aspects the same if they haven't changed, but you can also add to or replace some of the original aspects if they have changed.

Activity 4.4: Revisiting Your Self-Aspect Pie

Now redraw your pie below, even if it hasn't changed that much. Remember, like last time, the very important parts of you should be bigger slices of your pie and less important parts should be smaller.

Your self-aspect pie:

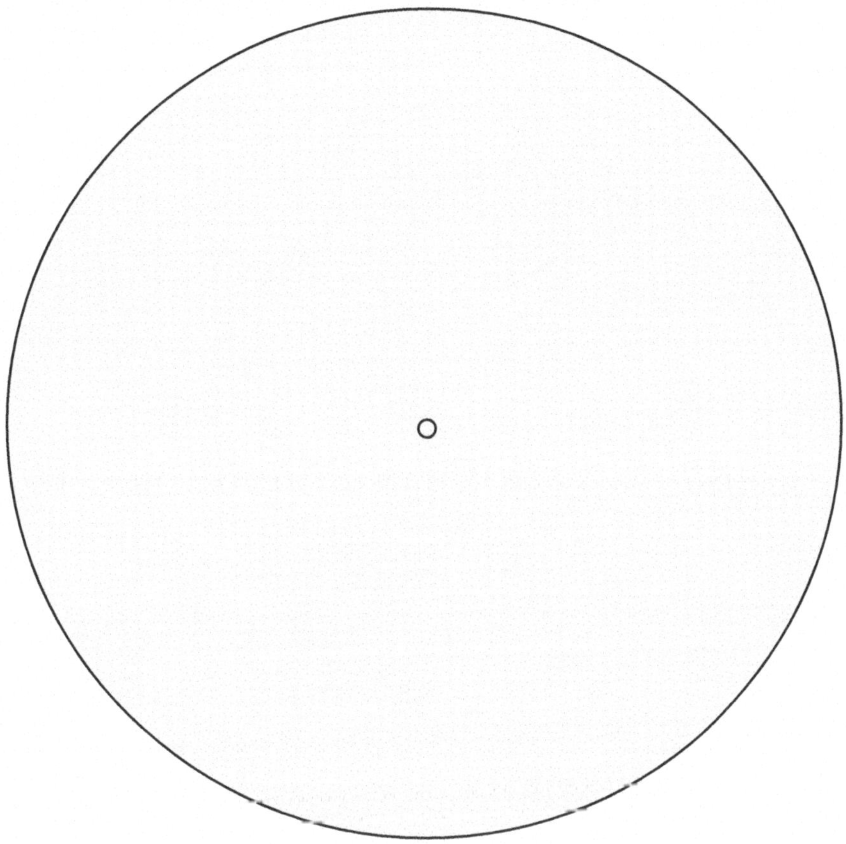

This self-aspect pie is a first step in thinking about which new groups to join and which existing groups to strengthen. It is useful because a group that fits with who you are—with your values, interests, and goals in life—is likely to be more meaningful and important to you and so will be one that you'll want to hang on to.

Now take a moment to consider how these important parts of you are "lived out" through your groups.

Revisiting your self-aspect pie

Are there important parts of yourself that are not currently represented by your groups?

What kind of groups could you join to live out the under-represented parts of you?

Activity 4.5: Choosing a New Group

Now, let's choose a new group to join. Write your ideas in the boxes below.

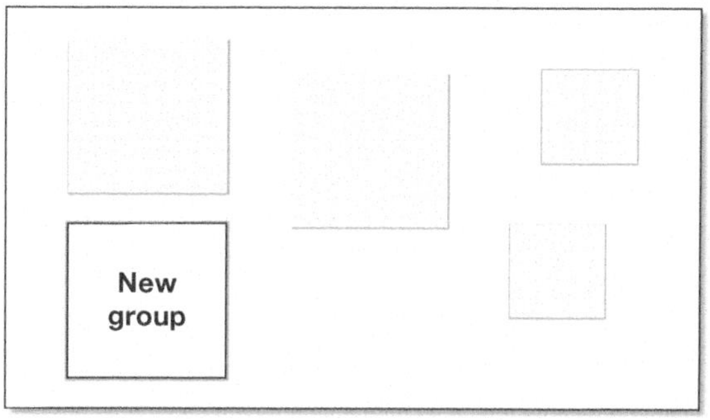

Choosing a new group

What new group would you like to connect with?

Why do you want to connect with this new group?

How can you connect with this new group?

Activity 4.6: Strengthening Existing Groups

Let's now think in the same way about how we might strengthen an existing group membership. Look back to your map to identify a group that you might want to engage with and see more.

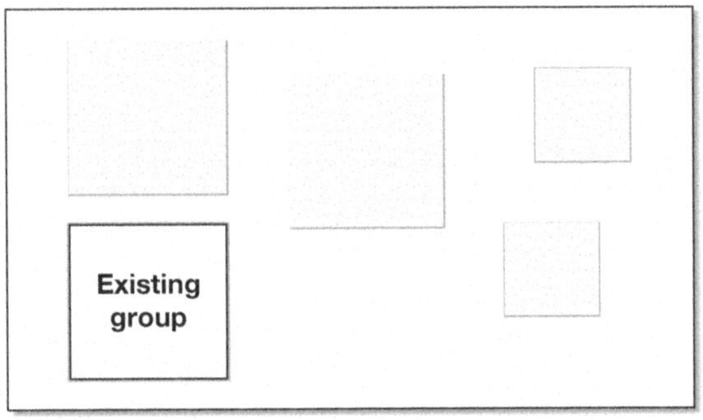

Strengthening an existing group

What existing group connection would you like to strengthen?

Why do you want to connect more to this group?

How will you be able to strengthen this connection?

Activity 4.7: A SMART Social Plan

To help you achieve your goals, it is a good idea to develop a **SMART** social plan. This plan needs to be:

Specific. You need to think about exactly what you are going to do.

Measurable. You need to be able to know that you've made progress.

Aligned. It needs to fit with how you see yourself (e.g., your values and priorities).

Realistic. You need to be able to make steady progress toward your goals.

Timely. You need to identify when exactly you are going to act on your plan, and you need to ensure you don't leave it too long before getting started.

The SMART plan is a way of getting people to think in more detail about the reality of their new group connections. By thinking through the different aspects of the plan, it becomes more achievable. Sometimes, however, it can be hard to know exactly how to make a SMART plan, so we have included an example below to help translate the ideas into reality.

An example SMART social plan:

Singing or music group.

My motivation to join:

This is important to me because singing is an important part of who I am and helps me to stay sane.

S *Find out what choirs or other music groups are out there locally.*

M *Commit to joining at least one of those groups.*

A *Group should focus on modern music.*

R *Choose a choir that meets only once a week.*

T *Attend the group at least once by the end of the month.*

A SMART social plan. In the first box below, choose a group from above that you want to make a part of your social plan—either an existing group to strengthen or a new group to join. Next, fill out the SMART details in your plan. This is what you will work on in the next month.

You will see some extra boxes and SMART details for you to return to at any point if you wish to extend or strengthen group ties in the future.

1. ____________________

S ______________________________
M ______________________________
A ______________________________
R ______________________________
T ______________________________

2. ____________________

S ______________________________
M ______________________________
A ______________________________
R ______________________________
T ______________________________

3. ____________________

S ______________________________
M ______________________________
A ______________________________
R ______________________________
T ______________________________

Keeping in Touch

You have all gained a group membership by participating in Groups 4 Health.

This group is a valuable resource that you have at your disposal right now—you have a roomful of people who are also interested in developing new social connections.

Take a moment now to find out whether others in the group would like to make contact during the break. There is space below to write down some contact details if you need.

Session Summary: Learning Points

As we did last time, let's finish by talking about some of the key learnings from today's session.

Activity 4.8: Learning Points from Today's Session

Note below the group's key learning points from today's session.

Learning points from today's session:

This reflection task is for you to complete before the next session.

Activity 4.9: Putting Your Social Plan into Action

You have already taken steps toward joining new groups, and you have created your own social plan that is achievable and SMART. Over the next few weeks, try carrying out your SMART plan. You can use the space below to note any barriers you face or successes you have. At our next session, we will talk together about what it has been like putting your social plan into action.

What barriers did you face when you were trying to carry out your social plan?	
What successes or positive experiences did you have?	
Would you do anything differently next time?	

CHAPTER 5 Session 5
Sustaining: Maintaining Groups

SESSION AIMS

1. To look at progress and troubleshoot managing our social groups.
2. To re-evaluate our social world and see how this compares to our original maps.
3. To wind down and say farewell.

Review and Check-In

Think about some of the positive experiences you have had in the process of managing your social world. Having positive experiences helps us feel better about ourselves, and this translates into positive health outcomes.

There is space below to jot down some of these experiences and thoughts as we talk this through.

....

....

....

....

Activity 5.1: Positive Experiences

So what were the positive experiences you had when putting your SMART plan into action? Write down some particularly enjoyable and memorable experiences below.

Positive experiences:

Troubleshooting

Sometimes things do not go according to plan or we might not manage our relationships with others the way we would like. This might have happened to you and others in the group since we last met. Let's review this as part of the next activity.

Activity 5.2: Strategies to Manage Challenges

In troubleshooting with the group, you'll come up with some strategies to overcome these challenges.

Use the space below to write down some challenges and then add strategies that you came up with or feel would be particularly useful for you.

Challenges experienced:

Strategies to manage challenges:

Returning to Your Social Identity Map

Our social relationships develop and change over time. This means it is likely that there have been some developments to your social identity map since you last created one (in Session 2). For this reason, it can be helpful to re-evaluate our social worlds to see how they might have changed, and creating a new social identity map is a good way of doing this.

Activity 5.3: Your New Social Identity Map

In the next exercise, you will create a new social identity map. You'll follow the same steps as last time, and all you need to do is complete each of the stages to create your new map. After you create this new map, you can compare it to your original to see whether things have changed.

Just like last time, you need to:

1. Write down the names of your groups on the different-sized Post-it Notes. Use larger Post-it Notes for more important groups and smaller Post-it Notes for less important groups.
2. In the **top left corner** rate how typical you are of each group (1–10).
3. In the **top right corner** indicate how many days in the month you do things with each group (0–30).
4. In the **bottom right corner** rate how much support you receive from each group (1–10).
5. In the **bottom left corner** rate how positive you feel about being a member of each group (1–10).
6. Use the distance between the Post-it Notes to show how similar or different your groups are.
7. Indicate with lines how easy it is to be a member of each of your groups at the same time (straight line = easy, wavy line = moderately easy, jagged line = hard). See the example below.

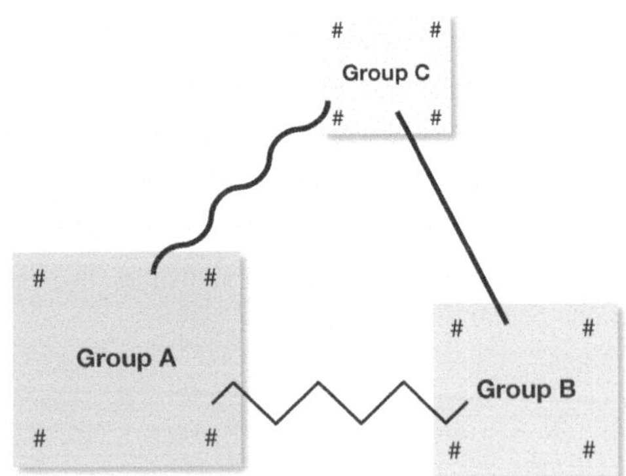

After creating your new social identity map, paste it here:

PLEASE FOLD YOUR COMPLETED MAP TO FIT THIS PAGE AND ATTACH IT HERE

Activity 5.4: Reflecting on Your Map

Looking at your new map, has anything changed about your groups?

Reflecting on your map

Activity 5.5: Checking on Your Goals

In the first session, you reflected on your goals for taking part in Groups 4 Health—look back at page 7.

Let's now take a moment together to reflect on whether we've achieved those goals. And, if not, what we could do to keep working on them?

Note down any good strategies that were discussed to help progress these goals.

Checking in on our goals

Take-Home Points

It's useful to think of the main take-home points from the entire program. Let's take a moment to reflect on these.

Activity 5.6: Groups 4 Health Take-Home Points

There is space below to jot down some notes as part of this activity.

Take-home points

Winding Down and Looking Ahead: Groups 4 Health as a Way of Life

Congratulations on taking part in Groups 4 Health! Through this program, we hope you have developed skills, strategies, and new ideas to help you manage your social groups and your social world. You will have written many of these things down in this Workbook, so it is a good idea to keep it handy as a record and a resource for the future.

We hope you enjoyed being a part of Groups 4 Health and that you have developed some skills and strategies along the way. Managing our social worlds is something that we'll all do throughout our lives, and we hope this program has given you some tools and resources that will help you to keep your networks alive and thriving into the future.

The manufacturer's authorised representative in the EU for product safety is Oxford University Press España S.A. of El Parque Empresarial San Fernando de Henares, Avenida de Castilla, 2 - 28830 Madrid (www.oup.es/en or product.safety@oup.com). OUP España S.A. also acts as importer into Spain of products made by the manufacturer.
Printed and bound by CPI Group (UK) Ltd, Croydon, CR0 4YY
14/09/2026
02216299-0001